EXPLORING DISUSED RAILWAYS IN EAST SCOTLAND

MICHAEL MATHER

Although most of the photographs I have presented here are my own, a big thank you must go to the following photographers who have made available photographs from their collections: Graeme Blair, David Crichton, Tony and Nick Harden, Graham Maxton, Bruce McCartney, Iain A. H. Smith, Hamish Stevenson and Kenneth G. Williamson. Thank you also to Julian Holland for the use of his map.

Extra thanks go to Graeme Blair for his help and encouragement and to Kenneth G. Williamson for his help in locating a particular photograph.

Rails Across The Border – A. J. Mullay – Patrick Stevens – 1990
BR Main Line Gradient Profiles – Ian Allan – 1997
Rail Centres Edinburgh – A. J. Mullay – Ian Allan – 1991
The Railways of Fife – William Scott Bruce – Melvin Press – 1980
Rail Scot website
Forgotten Relics website
Timetable World website

Final thanks to my daughter Katie for proofreading my manuscript.

Front cover image: Looking along the empty track bed of Leaderfoot Viaduct.
Back cover image: A surviving gradient post beside the Alva Branch.

First published 2017

Amberley Publishing
The Hill, Stroud
Gloucestershire, GL5 4EP

www.amberley-books.com

Copyright © Michael Mather, 2017

The right of Michael Mather to be identified as the Author of this work has been asserted in accordance with the Copyrights, Designs and Patents Act 1988.

ISBN 978 1 4456 5567 3 (print)
ISBN 978 1 4456 5568 0 (ebook)

British Library Cataloguing in Publication Data. A catalogue record for this book is available from the British Library.

Origination by Amberley Publishing.
Printed in the UK.

Introduction

Browsing most Ordnance Survey maps of East Scotland will show the legend 'Course of Old Railway'. In many areas, there are more of these than there are those in use. These closed lines, which were almost all opened in the nineteenth century, fell victim to increased road use and the need for the railways to make a profit.

When built, these lines were the equivalent of us today going into space, such was the difference in travelling time they made. Journeys that would have taken many hours or days could now be undertaken in a very short time, making it easier for people and goods to move quickly around the country.

This situation lasted for sixty or so years, until the advent of road transport – particularly after the First World War, when cars, lorries and buses became more prolific. Journeys, especially short ones, could be undertaken more quickly and cheaply by road than by rail.

This made the biggest difference to the shorter branch lines, which lost much of their passenger traffic. Indeed, some of these lines lost their passenger services as early as the 1920s, although most lasted into the 1950s and 1960s.

The Beeching Report in 1962 was the death knell for many lines – not just branches, but also for main lines too – and so, by the early 1970s, the railways in East Scotland were a shadow of their former selves.

Sad as this was (and there is now much regret that so many lines were closed, especially with today's busy roads, crowded trains and pollution), it was good news

This sign, erected in 2000 by the now disbanded Friends of Riccarton Junction, stands as a reminder of this famous junction. Behind stands the ruined station master's house. Today the junction and the remains of its platform are a fine stopping-off point for anyone walking the Waverley Route. (2016)

for walkers and cyclists, and so the rail traveller's loss became the walker's and cyclist's gain. The Scottish Right to Roam Act means that it is possible to explore these closed lines without hindrance – although there are still places that are out of bounds, e.g., where a track bed disappears under a cultivated field.

These closed lines, whether left undisturbed since closure, or converted into official or unofficial paths, provide relatively easy walking and cycling in the country, often far from roads. While most of the large railway infrastructure such as bridges, tunnels and stations is often still in place, it is the smaller things you may find, such as mile and gradient posts and signs, that add interest.

Wildlife also benefits from these closed lines, where both flora and fauna can flourish, undisturbed by traffic and field chemical sprays. In cities, too, closed lines are often turned into cycle tracks, providing a welcome oasis from the hustle and bustle of the city. It's surprising how much wildlife there is to see even on these city cycle paths.

Many farmers have utilised former railways as access tracks to their fields. These may be muddy to walk along, but at least there is no danger of them being over grown – just watch out for tractors!

Winter and early spring are often the best times to walk a line that has gone back to nature, as it is easier to get through any vegetation. However, beware in cuttings as, with no maintenance having been carried out to drainage systems, it can get very wet under foot. Care should also be taken when walking through tunnels; it's best not to go alone.

As already mentioned, Ordnance Survey maps are a good way of finding disused railways, but the up-to-date ones don't usually give the full picture. The National Library of Scotland website has Ordnance Survey maps from the 1920s available to view or download. These show all the lines as they were when they were open, complete with station names. They also show the amount of industrial lines there once was. Additionally, there are many books and websites where the curious can gather information.

In this volume, I have strived to show a selection of what can be found on and nearby these disused railways, and what I have presented here is just a small part of what is out there. It is aimed at not just the railway enthusiast, but also the walker, cyclist and anyone with a passing interest in any of these topics.

Throughout the text I have referred to the pre-Grouping (1923) railway companies – the Caledonian, North British and Great North of Scotland railways – as they either built or ultimately ran these lines. At the Grouping in 1923, the Caledonian became part of the London Midland & Scottish Railway, while the North British and Great North of Scotland became part of the London & North Eastern Railway. They all became part of the British Railways Scottish Region at nationalisation in 1948.

In recent months, following the success of the reopened Borders Railway, there have been calls for other disused lines to be considered for reopening, including some covered in this book, and also for converting more disused lines into cycle tracks – all of which can only be a good thing. Only time will tell.

Michael Mather
October 2016

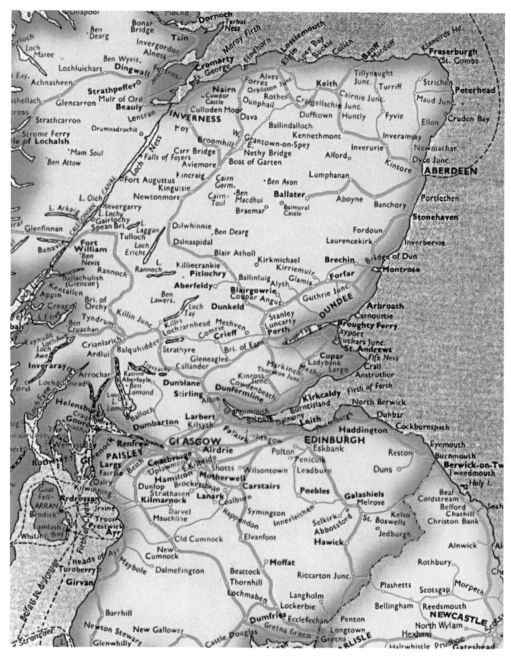

This British Railways Passenger Services map dates from 1950 and shows just how much of the country was served by rail at this time. All of the lines featured in this book, apart from the Fife & Kinross Railway, which had lost its passenger services that year, are on this map. (Julian Holland Collection)

The Formantine & Buchan Railway

This grandly named railway ran from Dyce Junction, on the Great North of Scotland Railway's Aberdeen to Keith line, to Maude Junction, where it split, with one line going to Peterhead via Mintlaw and the other to Fraserburgh via Strichen.

The railway opened in sections between 1861 and 1865 and came under the control of the Great North of Scotland Railway in 1866. Its main stations were at Ellon and Maude Junction, while there were also many country stations. The railway followed a winding switchback route that included some fairly steep gradients: trains leaving Fraserburgh, for instance, faced a near 6-mile climb after an initial level section, with some parts as steep as 1 in 70.

Principal traffic, after passengers, was fish from the ports of Peterhead and Fraserburgh. This, along with agricultural goods and produce from the Crosse & Blackwell factory at Peterhead, provided the railway with much of its revenue until road traffic and declining fish stocks took their toll.

Following the Beeching report, the line was earmarked for closure and passenger services were withdrawn in 1965. Peterhead's goods service lasted until 1970 and Fraserburgh's till 1979, when the whole line closed.

In 1981 Grampian Regional Council had the foresight to purchase the whole line from Dyce to Peterhead and Fraserburgh, and it has subsequently been turned into a walking and cycling path, now known as the Formantine and Buchan Way. This provides a 25-mile path from Dyce to Maude and then a choice of a further 15 miles to Fraserburgh or 13 miles to Peterhead, all through lovely agricultural countryside and with many access points where you can join or leave the route.

Half a mile before reaching Ellon station from the south, the path crosses the River Ythan by this fine viaduct – note the telegraph pole still attached. The Ythan rises at Ythan Wells and flows for 37 miles to Newburgh, 5 miles beyond Ellon, where it enters the North Sea. (2006)

At Ellon station, the stone-built water tank base, seen here, survives, as does the island platform. From Ellon, a branch line used to run to Boddam. It opened in 1897 and closed in 1945, and today most traces of it have disappeared, although the piers of a viaduct near Cruden Bay can still be seen. (2006)

The platforms at Auchnagatt station are surviving well and still sport the station name board supports. The main station building is in use as a home. (2006)

Maude Junction was where the trains split, with some going to Peterhead and others to Fraserburgh. The track bed nearest was for Fraserburgh, which was considered the main line, while the Peterhead line on the other side was thought of as the branch. The station is complete and in good order. It houses some small businesses and a small railway museum, which is open on the second weekend of each month from April to October (according to 2016 dates). At the far end of the large car park, the turntable pit can be found.

We shall now travel along the path to Fraserburgh. Soon after leaving Maude Junction, Fraserburgh trains faced a 3-mile climb at 1 in 70, with a small downhill and level section in the middle. This is the view looking down the gradient towards Maude. (2013)

Near Bruckley, milepost 32 ½ is slowly being strangled by a tree. Other mileposts remain on this route, all in better condition than this one. (2013)

A familiar sight at the line side was the surface men's huts, like this one built from railway sleepers. It now provides a welcome shelter for walkers or cyclists from the rain or the cold east wind that can blow in this area. (2013)

Philorth was the last station before Fraserburgh and was the private station of Lord Saltoun – hence the short platform. Like most of the country stations on the line, it is now a home. (2013)

These two photographs show the huge change that has taken place at Fraserburgh. The top photograph is from 1953, and shows just how large an area the railway took up. The bottom photograph from 2013 is of the former engine shed, seen to the left on the 1953 photograph. It is all that remains of the railway in Fraserburgh and is now used as a warehouse. There was once a turntable to the left of the shed. (1953 photograph – GNSRA/Graham Maxtone Collection)

Ballater

Ballater was the terminus of the Royal Deeside Railway, which ran from Aberdeen via Cults, Banchory, Lumphanan and Aboyne, following the River Dee to Banchory, where it turned northwest to Lumphanan before returning to the river route at Aboyne. The railway was opened to Ballater in 1866 and was operated by the Great North of Scotland Railway.

The station was provided with a goods yard and shed, and an engine shed with a turntable. There were plans to extend to Braemar, but Queen Victoria objected to this as it would pass close to Balmoral Castle. This didn't stop her, subsequent royals, and distinguished visitors from using the line to travel to Ballater and then on to Balmoral. A royal waiting room was even provided at Ballater station. Royal patronage didn't save the railway from closure, however, and in 1966 the last train ran, with the last royal train having run the year before.

Much of the railway can now be walked or cycled. The Deeside Way uses the track bed from Aberdeen to Coalford just beyond Petercoulter, Milton of Crathes to Banchory and Aboyne to Ballater. The present Royal Deeside Railway has relayed track from Milton of Crathes for 1 mile towards Banchory, while retaining the path. They now run services with steam and diesel locomotives.

Ballater station was restored as a visitor attraction with a restaurant, museum, tourist information centre, royal waiting room and a replica royal coach; however, sadly in 2015 it was completely destroyed by fire. Plans have now been submitted for a rebuild of the station in its original style.

Photographed in 1969, three years after the line closed, Ballater signal box still stands, with the home signal set at danger and the track overgrown. The levers were still in place, but the block instruments had been removed.

The top, 1969, photograph of Ballater shows that track had been lifted for the last few yards into the station, but track remained in place along the rest of the line at this time. Note milepost 43 on the platform. Not only have the tracks been lost in the bottom, 2012, photograph, but so has the view of the hills.

Ballater's Royal station was a superb sight and was well worth a visit. Opened in 2008 by Prince Charles, it was a major tourist attraction in the area. Hopefully in the not-too-distant future, the rebuilt station will be welcoming visitors again. (2012)

This replica of Queen Victoria's Royal Coach, in which she travelled to Ballater in 1869, stands in the station platform. The original is at the National Railway Museum at York. The coach was commissioned by Visit Scotland following a suggestion by Prince Charles, and was funded by the National Lottery. The beautiful interior is shown in the lower photograph, the figures being Queen Victoria and one of her daughters, complete with a black Labrador. The fire service was able to save the coach in the 2015 fire. (2012)

The Speyside (Whisky) Railway

Running through scenic country, the Speyside Railway opened between Nethy Bridge and Dufftown in 1863, where it connected with the Keith & Dufftown Railway, which had opened in 1862. A further section opened in 1866 between Nethy Bridge and Boat of Garten, where it joined the Highland Railway's line from Forres to Aviemore, the two lines running parallel for the last 4 miles from Tullochgorum to Boat of Garten. The line was operated by the Great North of Scotland Railway.

At Craigellachie there was also a junction with a line going to Elgin. Two short branch lines, both to serve distilleries, ran from Cromdale to Ballmenach and Carron to Dailuaine, each having their own steam locomotives. There are many towns and distilleries along the route, and the whisky industry provided much traffic for the railway until road transport took over.

The route from Boat of Garten to Craigellachie was closed to passengers in 1965 and that from Craigellachie to Keith in 1968. Freight services didn't last much longer, with Boat of Garten to Aberlour closing in 1968 and Aberlour to Dufftown in 1971. The Dufftown to Keith line remained open until 1991 and is now run as a preserved railway using diesel multiple units.

The Speyside Way long-distance path uses the track bed of the old line from Craigellachie to Balindalloch, a short section near Cromdale, and from Granton on Spey to Nethy Bridge – it's a great walk or cycle. The line can also be walked from Craigellachie to Dufftown to meet up with the Keith & Dufftown Railway. Care should be taken cycling this part, as there have been a number of landslips.

Nearing the southern end of the Speyside Railway, two British Railways Class 24s, D5070 and D5127, approach Tullochgorum at the head of the eighteen-coach Grand Scottish Rail Tour on 25 March 1967. (David Crichton)

My wife and daughter take in the view to the River Spey from this fine viewpoint beside the path. (1987)

Standing adjacent to Tamdhu Distillery is Knockando station and signal box. At the time this photograph was taken in 1987, the station was acting as the distillery's visitor centre. Since then, the distillery has closed, changed owners and reopened again, but is no longer open to visitors. The station was renovated in 2012 and has been offered to the local community.

This cast-iron London & North Eastern Railway trespass notice near Carron has seen better days. Once a common sight beside the railway, they are now collector's items. (2012)

At Carron station, which stands disused but in solid condition, time stands still on this rusted old clock and the water fountain remains dry. Many of the stations on Speyside were fitted with this design of fountain. (2012)

Dailuaine Halt is near to the distillery of the same name, and the short platform is about the length of one carriage. It has a handy picnic table, which is fine for a break. Sadly, since this photograph was taken, the sign has been removed and the platform has been deteriorating. (2012)

This was Dailuaine Distillery engine shed. The distillery had its own steam locomotive, which had the rare distinction of being one of the few industrial locomotives that were permitted to venture onto British Railways track. This it did on trip workings to nearby Carron station. The locomotive survives and is on display at Aberfeldy Distillery – see page 40. (2012)

Approaching Craigellachie, the path crosses this short bridge, perched high above the River Spey, and then enters the short Taminurie Tunnel. (2012)

At Craigellachie, the path leaves the River Spey and follows the River Fiddich, crossing the river soon after leaving the station. After a 2-mile climb, it crosses the river again at this viaduct and climbs on towards Dufftown. (2012)

Closed level-crossing gates are pictured beside the now-silent Colvalmore Distillery on the outskirts of Dufftown. The distillery, which opened in 1894, was rebuilt following a fire in 1909 and continued in production until 1985. The buildings are now used to store Glenfiddich and Balvenie whiskies. (2015)

The path ends at Dufftown station, where you can board the train for the leisurely 11-mile trip to Keith. The railway uses diesel multiple units, which are ideal for viewing the stunning scenery and counting the distilleries. The line ends just beyond Keith Town station, but there are plans to reconnect to Network Rail's tracks at Keith station. (2015)

The Dundee & Newtyle Railway

When it was opened in 1831, this was one of Scotland's first railways. Built to a 4 foot 6 inch gauge, and later changed to standard gauge, it featured three inclined plains: one in Dundee, a second at Balbeuchly and the other immediately south of Newtyle.

Stationary steam engines hauled trains up the inclined plains and, for the first two years of operation, horses were used as haulage along the leveller sections before steam locomotives took over in 1833. This method of operation was limiting and time consuming, and so in the 1860s diversionary routes, avoiding the inclined plains, were opened to allow locomotives with longer trains to work the whole route.

Trains that had left from Dundee Ward Road station, then travelling up the first inclined plain, before going through a tunnel under the Law Hill, now left from the Caledonian Railway's Dundee West station, heading west to Ninewells Junction, where they turned off for Lochee and then north to Newtyle.

The diversionary route at Newtyle rendered the original station redundant as a passenger station, with a replacement being built on the new route. The original station was connected to the new line and used for goods only. Beyond Newtyle, two lines ran parallel before splitting, with one going to Ardler junction for Blairgowrie and Perth, and the other to Alyth junction for Alyth and Aberdeen.

Passenger services were withdrawn in 1955, and the line closed in 1965. Parts of the line are now official paths, these being from Achray to North Dronley and the Newtyle diversion, and the track bed towards Ardler Junction.

This is the south end of Newtyle station, one of the oldest stations in Scotland. From here, trains going to Dundee were hauled up the Hatton incline by the stationary engine at the top, before continuing under their own power. (2013)

The north end of Newtyle station. It was from this end that goods traffic arrived and left, following the opening of the diversionary route and the building of a new station at Newtyle. Trains leaving here travelled north for a short distance before joining the lines to Alyth and Ardler Junction. (2013)

Climbing the Newtyle diversion – it was both steep and on a sharp curve. It is now a secluded path. (2013)

This sign provides the walker with information on the former railway. Dronley station, below, was on the new line avoiding the Balbeuchly incline and was built over a bridge, hence the fencing. This is the view looking towards Dundee. (2016)

The Strathmore Route
and its Branches

Mention the Strathmore Route to any railway enthusiast who remembers the 1960s, and they will probably think of A4 Pacific steam locomotives. It was on this relatively straight and easily graded line that these thoroughbreds of the East Coast Main Line were able to stretch their legs in their final years, while working the Glasgow–Aberdeen 3-hour expresses, covering for the new diesels that weren't up to the job.

Fully open by 1848, this 45-mile Caledonian Railway line ran from Stanley Junction on the Highland Main Line to Kinnaber Junction on the east coast. Running through largely agricultural land, the only towns of any size were Couper Angus and Forfar. Although it did have many country stations, the lack of major towns on the route probably brought about its downfall. Blairgowrie, Alyth, Kirriemuir and Brechin were all connected by branches, as well as the line from Dundee via Newtyle.

The line was closed to passengers in 1967 and singled between Stanley Junction and Forfar, with passenger trains being re-routed via Dundee. The route from Forfar to Bridge of Dunn was closed completely, while Kinnaber Junction to Bridge of Dunn and the Brechin Branch remained open for freight until closure in 1981. The following year Stanley Junction to Forfar closed too. A sad end to what, in today's crowded railway, could have been a useful high-speed line.

Buildings, roads and agriculture have covered over parts of the track bed, but much remains, although none of it has been turned into an official path. Some parts can be walked, such as that from Ardler to Alyth Junction for instance. Bridge of Dunn to Brechin has reopened as the Caledonian Railway, and services are run at weekends using steam and diesel locomotives.

The name board on the signal box says Stanley Junction, but it is a junction no more. The gap in the trees denotes where the Strathmore Route once ran. (2010)

Shortly after leaving Stanley, the line crossed the River Tay on the Ballathie Viaduct at Cargill. This 200-yard structure opened in 1848 and originally had five 100-foot wooden arch spans, but these were replaced with steel in 1890 to allow the passage of heavier trains. (2013)

The site of Ardler Junction, where the line from Newtyle joined the Strathmore Route: the route of the main line can be seen passing between the trees, while the line from Newtyle was to the right. A serious accident occurred here in 1948, when a train coming down from Newtyle failed to stop at a signal and collided with a passing postal train travelling at 70 mph. (2013)

The level-crossing keeper's hut at Camno Crossing still survives, as does his house. This was one of many level crossings on this line. (2013)

Taken from a DMU rail tour approaching the Ardler Junction distant signal in 1980, the embankment of the Newtyle to Alyth junction line, which has since been removed, is on the left. To this day, the telegraph poles, complete with wires and the signal post (minus arms), survive. The track bed here is now quite overgrown, but still passable. (Graeme Blair)

The Ardler Junction distant signal post reaches for the sky. Why this wasn't removed after the track was lifted is a mystery! (2015)

A4 Pacific No. 60009 *Union of South Africa* takes water at Forfar station while working a Glasgow–Aberdeen express in 1965. Nothing remains of Forfar station today. (Author's collection)

Forfar engine shed, which closed in 1964, now stands in the middle of an industrial estate. The shed had four tracks and was a sub shed of Perth. Now in industrial use, it is in excellent condition and has been re-roofed. (2013)

Auldbar Road station is probably the most complete closed station left on the line. As seen here, the station building, signal box (now a summer house), and loading bank survive, as do the platforms, which are out of sight behind the bushes. The station closed to passengers in 1956. (2013)

The Guthrie Gate is also a railway bridge, carrying the Strathmore Route across the entrance to Guthrie Castle. Dating back to 1468 and home to the Guthrie family up until the 1980s, the castle is now a venue for weddings, corporate events and occasional open days. (2015)

At Glasterlaw, one set of level-crossing gates are still in place and the repositioned home signal is sited where the signal box used to be. No trace of the railway can be seen on the other side of the road. The gates and signal are part of a private residence. (2015)

Bridge of Dunn station, which closed to passengers in 1967, is now the southern terminus of the Caledonian Railway. Class 27 D5370 stands with its train on what used to be the Down main line, waiting to leave for Brechin. (2015)

The 6-mile Blairgowrie Branch opened in 1855, running from Couper Angus to Blairgowrie. Trains crossed this viaduct across the River Isla soon after leaving Couper Angus. The remains of an embankment can be seen beyond, but most traces of the line have gone. Trains ran from Dundee to Blairgowrie via Newtyle and Ardler Junction. (2010)

Hidden in the trees beside the A923, at a point where the railway crossed the road by a level crossing, is the platform of Rosemount station. In its heyday, the branch was kept busy with jute, soft fruit and tourist traffic. It closed to passengers in 1955 and freight in 1965. (2015)

This was the original Meigle station on the 8-mile Alyth Branch, which ran from Alyth Junction. The station was situated beside a level crossing and was replaced by a wooden one on the other side of the road, which hasn't survived. The branch opened in 1861 and had a direct connection with Dundee via Newtyle. It closed to passengers in 1951 and freight in 1965. (2015)

Leaving the main line at Kirriemuir Junction, 2 miles west of Forfar, the Kirriemuir Branch terminated here at what is now a small housing estate, still retaining the station platform. Only 2 miles long, the branch opened in 1854. Passenger services were withdrawn in 1952 and freight in 1965. (2015)

The Aberfeldy Branch

The Highland Railway's Aberfeldy Branch, which opened in 1865, left the Highland Main Line at Ballinluig and was 8 miles in length. Soon after leaving Ballinluig, the line crossed the rivers Tummel and Tay on two similar viaducts, of which only the Tay Viaduct survives. Only two intermediate stations were provided, with one at Balnaguard Platform, which didn't open until 1935, and one at Grandtully.

Much of the goods traffic on the line would have been to and from Dewars Whisky Distillery at Aberfeldy, which the line ran alongside. Aberfeldy and its surrounding area is a popular tourist destination, and this would have generated passenger traffic; however, it couldn't have been enough as the line was closed completely in 1965.

Parts of the line are passable: crossing the Tay Viaduct at Logierait, one can walk along the track bed to Balnaguard Platform without any hindrance, as much of the route is used as a farm track. A path leads from Grandtully to Aberfeldy, using the track bed as far as where the line crossed the A827; from here it follows the River Tay. This path can flood when the river is high, and the walker has to take to the main road. For those following the railway, it is better to be on the road, as both run parallel for the last mile into Aberfeldy.

The Grade A-listed Tay Viaduct at Logierait spans a swollen River Tay on the day this photograph was taken. The viaduct consists of two 137-foot spans and is cared for by the local community. (2015)

The viaduct at Logierait is in superb condition and is open to pedestrians and light vehicles. From here to Balnaguard Platform, it is a pleasant 2½-mile walk. (2015)

Beware of tractors! Yes, there may not be any trains, but tractors come this way. The driver of this one had time to stop for a chat and told us of the community involvement with the viaduct. (2015)

In the village of Balnaguard this LMS sign still points the way to Balnaguard Platform. Although it is broken, by reading both sides you get the picture. (2015)

The site of Balnaguard Platform is now a silage pit and beyond the bridge the track bed has been ploughed up. Prominent behind is the 2,559-foot-high Faragon Hill. Meanwhile, one of the local residents looks on. (2015)

At Grandtully, the station site is now a car park and base for white-water canoeists on the nearby River Tay. The goods loading bank seen here is now part of a caravan and camping site. (2015)

Leaving Grandtully, the path winds uphill through the trees with glimpses of the River Tay. A detour up a short climb takes the walker to this fine viewpoint, looking down onto the river. (2015)

Approaching Aberfeldy, the line passed by Dewars Whisky Distillery, where this 1939 Andrew Barclay 0-4-0 steam locomotive is on display. It was formerly named *Dailuaine* and worked at the distillery of the same name on Speyside. (2015)

With the overgrown railway embankment in the right foreground, it can clearly be seen how close the line passed to the distillery. Opened by John Dewar & Sons in 1898, the distillery draws its water from the nearby Pitilie Burn. The distillery is open to the public and is well worth a visit. (2016)

British Railways Class 24 D5125 stands at Aberfeldy station with its one-coach train for Ballinluig in 1964. (Robin Barbour collection, courtesy of Bruce McCartney)

The station site today is now a car park, seen in the distance here. This viewpoint was chosen so as to include the houses on the hill, as seen in the 1964 photograph. (2016)

Lochearnhead, St Fillans & Comrie Railway

Built at great expense because of the terrain it crossed, this 15-mile railway opened between 1901 and 1905 and linked the Crieff & Comrie Railway with the Callander & Oban, which joined this line at Balquhidder Junction. All were operated by the Caledonian Railway.

The promoters of the line had high hopes of transporting both large amounts of freight from Oban to the east coast and also tourists, both of which failed to materialise. The area it passed through was never going to be able to generate enough traffic on its own.

Stations were provided at Dalchonzie Halt, St Fillans and Lochearnhead. Many bridges and viaducts were required, especially on the St Fillans to Lochearnhead section, where it traversed the hillside above Loch Earn. Concrete was used extensively on all of these structures, but was finished to look like stone.

After less than fifty years' service, the line closed to freight in 1950 and to passengers the following year. However, the track was retained for occasional use in connection with the building of the Glen Lednock hydro-electric scheme. It finally closed in 1959.

The track bed has lain pretty much undisturbed with almost all the bridges intact since then, but recently a scheme titled the Loch Earn Railway Path has been set up to turn the route into a cycle path. A short section is already in place between Balquhidder and Lochearnhead. The plan is to have a cycle path running all the way from Comrie to Lochearnhead, linking up with the Glen Ogle route.

Since the photographs that follow were taken, work on this scheme has moved on briskly and some parts are already surfaced.

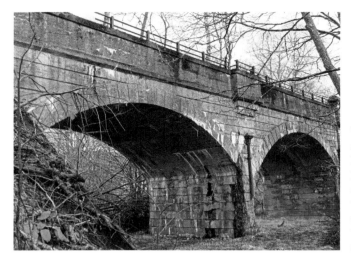

These two arches standing on the west bank of the River Earn are all that remain of a lengthy viaduct that crossed a large part of Comrie. The viaduct crossed the river and the A85 on steel spans, the rest being concrete arches. (2015)

Dalchonzie Halt was the first station after Comrie. It was also known as Dalchonzie platform or siding, which is what the name boards called it. It had a wooden platform and was a request stop. Unusually, the signal box was attached to the station building, which is now a home. The signal box controlled a level crossing. (2014)

Heading west from Dalchonzie, the track bed passes through this rock cutting and then makes its third crossing of the River Earn, which it crosses again at Tynrioch on a similar bridge. (2014)

Two views of St Fillans station: the top, undated, was taken when the line was open. Today the station is part of a caravan site and still retains many of its original features, including the signal box, the roof of which can be seen here. If visiting the station, please make yourself known to the owners, who are very welcoming and happy to show people round. (2014) (Historic photograph – Tony & Nicky Harden collection)

Shortly after St Fillans station, the track bed passes through this short tunnel. It is gated at each end at the moment, but hopefully it will soon be possible to pass through.

The task of replacing the missing bridge across the Glen Tarken Burn was the first project undertaken by the Loch Earn Railway Path group, this being the only bridge to have been removed along Loch Earn side.

Some stunning views across Loch Earn can be seen. The snow-covered peak is Ben Our, 2,400 feet high.

All along the track side there are remains of fallen telegraph poles; this is the only one still standing, complete with wires hanging from it. Such is nature and the passage of time that a nearby tree has grown around the wires.

One of the many viaducts along the track, but one of the few that it is possible to photograph, due to the steepness of the ravines that many of them cross.

Lochearnhead station is in superb condition and is owned by the Hertfordshire Scouts Association, who use it as an outdoor centre. Like St Fillans station, the owners are very welcoming to visitors, but announce your presence first.

The Railway Through Glenfarg

This railway, which passed across and through the Ochil Hills, was opened by the North British Railway in 1890, the same year as the Forth Bridge, thus providing a direct route between Edinburgh and Perth. The line was steeply graded and ran between Mawcarse Junction on the Fife & Kinross Railway, and Bridge of Earn on the Ladybank to Hilton Junction line.

Travelling north, trains climbed at 1 in 94 after leaving Mawcarse and, on passing Glenfarg summit, dropped steeply down at a 1-in-75 gradient across two viaducts and through two tunnels in Glenfarg to Bridge of Earn, and then on to Perth via Hilton Junction and Moncrieffe Tunnel. The 1-in-75 climb from Bridge of Earn presented a challenge for steam locomotives and their crews, especially when passing through the two 500-yard tunnels; the exhaust from the slow-moving locomotives made breathing difficult, and they would be glad to get to out into the fresh air!

The line was never earmarked for closure in the Beeching proposals, but in 1970 it was nevertheless closed, as part of the route was required for the new M90 motorway, which opened a few years later. Thankfully the most interesting part of the route wasn't touched by the motorway – namely the viaducts and tunnels in Glenfarg itself – and it is possible to walk all the way through. Access can be gained by heading south from the Bein Inn on the B996, a short distance after passing under the viaduct.

Following the route of the railway, this is the M90, to the north of Glenfarg village. The truck and buses are nearly at the summit of the climb from Bridge of Earn.

Two views taken from roughly the same spot, looking towards the south viaduct and tunnel mouth. In the top view from June 1970, six months after closure, the tracks are still in place, but the fishplates have been removed from the Up line, ready for lifting. Meanwhile, in the bottom view from 2012, nature has taken over.

Glenfarg South Viaduct spans the River Farg and the B996, formerly the A90, before the opening of the motorway. The viaduct is still owned by British Railways, as denoted by the white stencil above the crash barrier. It was recently refurbished, with stonework replaced and a new waterproof membrane laid on the track bed. (2010)

The south tunnel, unusually for the time, was concrete lined. This was the straighter of the two tunnels and so isn't completely dark inside. (2012)

Left: A water culvert under the track bed, still doing its job. Note the brick-lined bed. (2012)
Right: With the north tunnel behind, Jules Hathaway holds a lump of coal found at the trackside that had almost certainly fallen from a steam locomotive at least twenty-three years before this photograph was taken in 1990.

The north tunnel is on a curve and totally dark in the centre. It is lined with a mixture of stone, brick and concrete. A local farmer sometimes uses it as a store. (2012)

Left: A refuge built into the wall of the north tunnel for track workers to go into when a train was passing. *Right*: This faded and rusty bridge plate is fixed to the north portal of the north tunnel. (2012)

Passengers on trains exiting the north tunnel got this super view looking across Strath Earn towards Kirkton Hill to the left and Moncrieffe Hill to the right. (2012)

Surrounded by trees, the very-difficult-to-photograph north viaduct is reflected in this nearby pond. As it doesn't cross a main road, it doesn't receive the care the south viaduct receives. (2012)

The Fife & Kinross Railway

Opened in 1857/8, this 14-mile line ran from Ladybank on the North British main line through Fife, to Kinross. It terminated at a temporary station called Hopefield (Kinross) and was single line throughout.

Two years afterwards, in 1860, the Kinross-shire Railway opened, running from Lumphinnans, on the Dunfermline to Thornton line, to Kinross. The two lines joined at what would become Kinross Junction station when the Devon Valley Railway opened in 1863.

Intermediate stations were Auchtermuchty, Strathmiglo, Gateside, Mawcarse and Milnathort. Mawcarse became a junction with the opening of the Glenfarg Route in 1890, when the line was doubled from Lumphannans through to Mawcarse and on to Glenfarg. A new Kinross Junction station was opened at this time too.

Passenger services on the line were an early casualty, being withdrawn between Ladybank and Mawcarse in 1950, although Mawcarse remained open to passengers until 1964, as did Milnathort. Freight was withdrawn between Ladybank and Auchtermuchty in 1957, and this part of the line was then used to store redundant wagons and coaches. The line closed completely as far as Mawcarse in 1964.

The remaining part of the Fife & Kinross Railway from Mawcarse to Kinross closed in 1970, following the closure of the Glenfarg Route. Almost all trace of the line between Ladybank and Auchtermuchty has gone, as has that from Burnside to Mawcarse and Arlary, and from Milnathort to Kinross. Between Auchtermuchty and Burnside parts are passable, including from Gateside Mills to Gateside, which is an official path, and from Arlary to Milnathort, which is a surfaced cycle track.

The buffer stops in the Fife & Kinross Railway bay platform at Ladybank station are still in place. They are now part of a community garden. (2016)

The crew and a station porter stand beside a Sentinel steam railcar that is standing at the bay platform at Ladybank station in 1938. These railcars were used on the Fife & Kinross line at this time. (Alexander Wilson – Iain A. H. Smith collection)

Auchtermuchty station façade and platform survive, built into the office building of the Sterling Furniture warehouse. Originally Rippin Structures started business in the station goods shed, before building the shed seen on the right, which extends along the track bed. Two other stations survive, at Strahmiglo and Gateside, and both are now houses. (2016)

Still owned by British Railways, Bridge 17 once carried a road into Strathmiglo, but road improvements have rendered it redundant. It is now only an access road to fields, but can still be walked or cycled over. (2011)

Heading west from Strathmiglo, still fenced off, the track bed is initially clear to walk, but bushes hamper progress a little further on. (2011)

Progress beyond Strathmiglo is finally halted by this missing bridge across the River Eden, the first of seven crossings of the river by the railway. This is one of three steel-built bridges that were removed after the closure of the line. (2011)

Corston Tower, built in the sixteenth century, stands beside the line. Originally a residence of the Ramsay family, before passing to the Colquhouns, it all but collapsed in 1882, leaving just the one wall standing. The West Lomond Hill looms behind; it is the highest hill in Fife at 1,713 feet. (2011)

The next crossing of the River Eden is by this fine stone bridge. There are another two similar bridges between here and Gateside Mills. On the pathway from Gateside Mills to Gateside station, a missing steel bridge has been replaced by a wooden one. (2011)

The site of Mawcarse Junction is barely recognisable as having been a railway. The Fife & Kinross line approached beside the fence on the right, while the Glenfarg line curved away to the left. (2012)

All that remains of Mawcarse station is the goods loading bank. (2012)

The Devon Valley Railway

Twenty years in the building, the single-line Devon Valley Railway opened in stages between 1851 and 1871, running between Kinross Junction and Alloa, via Dollar and Tillicoultry. The Alloa to Tillicoultry section opened first, followed by Kinross to Rumbling Bridge, and then Tillicoultry to Dollar, leaving the most difficult section in the middle until last. This involved building viaducts over the Gairney Burn and the River Devon, east of Dollar. The Devon viaduct required a long approach embankment. At Arndean an 80-foot-deep cutting through a hill of sand also had to be dug.

Stations were provided at Balado, Crook of Devon, Rumbling Bridge, Dollar and Tillicoultry.

The line was operated by the North British Railway and services included Perth–Glasgow trains after the Glenfarg route opened in 1890. It also saw use as a diversionary route.

Passenger services ended in 1964 and the Dollar to Kinross Junction section was closed completely at this time. Alloa to Dollar remained open for coal traffic from Dollar Mine until the mine closed in 1973.

Following closure of the last section, the Scottish Railway Preservation Society looked seriously into taking it over to run as a preserved line, but this was never carried out. This wasn't the end of the story, however, as the Dollar to Alloa section is now a cycle track.

Other parts can also be explored, including in the Arndean, Vicar's Bridge area, where it is possible to walk to the Dollar Viaduct and almost to the Gairney Burn Viaduct. However, this can't be completed as one walk because a bridge over a road has been removed near Vicar's Bridge.

This platform edge is all that remains of the once-busy Kinross Junction station, which closed in 1970. Much of the site is now buried under the M90, visible in the background. The platform once had an ornamental pond in the shape of Loch Leven, complete with islands. (2015)

The line climbed for most of the way from Alloa to Kinross, including 4 miles at 1 in 70 east of Dollar. This view, east of Crook of Devon, shows the line still climbing towards Kinross. Note the old sleeper in the foreground. The summit of West Lomond can be seen in distance. (2015)

The site of Rumbling Bridge station is now a small housing development, with the track bed used as an access road. One platform has been retained and is kept in an attractive state. (2015)

The lofty five-arch Gairnie Burn Viaduct spans a steep-sided gorge. It is hidden by trees from all around, but can be reached by walking up the Craigton farm road from Powmill, from where the track bed to the viaduct can be accessed. (2015)

Looking down to the Gairnie Burn from the viaduct. Out of site in the trees is the River Devon into which the Gairnie Burn flows, downstream from where the Devon falls 40 feet at Cauldron Linn. (2015)

Constructed of sleepers and rails, this shoring is holding back an embankment that must have started moving at some time when the line was still open. The rails are now being bent by the force of a tree growing behind the sleepers. (2015)

A Railway Society of Scotland DMU rail tour calls at Dollar station in 1968, four years after the last regular passenger train ran on the line. The rail tour also took in the Strathmore Route to Forfar, which had closed to passengers the previous year.

Meanwhile in 2015, only one man and his dog are passing through the station. The surfaced cycle track starts shortly after the station.

The cycle track curves away downhill towards Tillicoultry. The post on the right would once have held gradient boards, indicating a change in gradient at this point. (2015)

The impressive brick-built abutment and piers of Tillicoultry Viaduct, which spanned the meandering River Devon. The steel spans have long since been removed, as have the abutment and embankment on the other side of the river. At Tillicoultry station, the cycle track takes a detour to avoid this gap, rejoining the track bed in the trees at the far side of the field. (2015)

The Caledonian Line to Leith

This double-track line, which opened in 1861, started off as the Granton Branch. It ran from Dalry Road Junction on the Caledonian Railway's main line out of Princes Street station, crossing the North British main line at Haymarket, then on to Granton Docks and Gas Works. The line to Leith Docks turned off the Granton Branch at Crewe Junction and opened to freight in 1864. Passenger services started to run from Princes Street to Leith North in 1879, following the building of a short spur from Newhaven Junction to Leith North station. Four tracks ran from Newhaven Junction, two to the docks and two to Leith North.

Stations on the line were at: Dalry Road; Murrayfield; Craigleith, where a line branched off to Barnton; East Pilton, which opened in 1934; Granton Road; Newhaven; and Leith North, as opposed to the North British North Leith station!

Diesel multiple units were introduced on the line in its last years but these didn't generate enough traffic. Consequently passenger services were withdrawn in 1962 and the line closed in 1967.

The line from Haymarket to Leith is now a cycle track, one of many of Edinburgh's former railways to have been treated this way. Road realignment and industrial units now cover the site of Leith North station. If the Edinburgh tram project had continued with the original plans, the line would have had trams running on it from Leith to Haymarket to join up with the link out to Edinburgh Airport – but this wasn't to be.

A short walk from Haymarket station, the path to Leith begins by climbing the embankment, which once led the line onto the bridge across the North British main line. (2015)

Climbing up the path, the walker gets a good view of the tram line to the airport and Haymarket depot, once the home of LNER Pacifics and Deltics. (2015)

Approaching Murrayfield station, of which the platforms survive, the path crosses Roseburn Terrace, seen here with one of Edinburgh's buses approaching. Murrayfield station was the first home of the Scottish Railway Preservation Society. (2015)

Barnton Junction, immediately north of Craigleith station, was where the line to Davidson Mains and Barnton branched off, and now also a cycle path, seen here branching off to the left. The Barnton line opened in 1894, closed to passengers in 1951, and closed completely in 1960. (2016)

Not wishing to condone graffiti, I thought this worth including as, on a visit some months later, these pictures had gone and had been replaced with other works of art! The bridge that carries Telford Road over the path seems to be a favourite place for graffiti artists. (2015)

East Pilton Halt, built to serve the Bruce Peebles transformer factory on the left and the Northern General Hospital on the right, didn't open until 1934. It is seen in the undated top photograph. Today the factory, destroyed by fire in 1999, has been replaced with housing, while the hospital site is now a supermarket, leaving only the bridge recognisable. (2016) (Historic photograph – Kenneth G. Williamson – Hamish Stevenson collection)

Clark Road Bridge, which crosses the path, is finished in Scottish Region blue and has this interesting brick infill between the steel beams. (2015)

Newhaven station is the only station to survive on the line and is in commercial use. Like Craigleith and Granton Road stations, it is at road level and at right angles to the line. (2015)

Now on to what was the four-track section of the line approaching Leith. This is Newhaven Road Bridge, again finished in Scottish Region blue. The path follows what was the passenger line to Leith North, while the overgrown part is where the goods lines to Leith Docks once were. (2015)

The end of the line, with the path in the distance climbing up to the main road, which the bridge in the foreground once carried. (2015)

Scotland Street to Granton

Most people shopping in the Princes Street Mall in Edinburgh will have no idea that, deep beneath their feet, are the remains of a railway station and the portal of a tunnel that stretches for 1,000 yards north under Edinburgh's New Town.

Canal Street station, which opened in 1847, sat at right angles to the present Waverley station and trains departed from it north down the 1-in-27 gradient of Scotland Street Tunnel, bound for Granton. The gradient was too steep for locomotives, and so brake coaches were used going down the hill, while a stationary engine pulled trains up into the station.

This was the main line out of Edinburgh to Fife and Dundee. Once passengers had reached Granton, they transferred to the train ferry to take them across the Firth of Forth to Burntisland, where they continued their journey north by rail.

In 1868 the North British Railway built a new line via Abbeyhill to avoid Scotland Street Tunnel, meaning trains for Granton left Waverley station heading east, before taking the new line, which joined the original route at Trinity Junction. Canal Street station and Scotland Street Tunnel were then closed, with the line up from Granton terminating at what became Scotland Street coal depot. This line closed in 1967 and is now a cycle path from Scotland Street to Trinity station. All trace of the line beyond Trinity to Granton has now gone.

The north portal of Scotland Street Tunnel. Since it closed in 1868, it has been used as a mushroom farm, and an air-raid shelter and emergency control centre for LNER staff during the Second World War. The ground level has been raised since the coal depot closed. (2015)

Scotland Street coal depot, which sat between Scotland Street and Rodney Street tunnels, is now a play park. The portal of Rodney Street Tunnel can just be seen behind the branches. (2015)

The path crosses the Water of Leith at Warriston Viaduct and this is the view that travellers would have had from the train, looking up to Edinburgh Castle. Although it wouldn't have been so clear, as 'Auld Reekie' would have been at its smokiest in the nineteenth century! (2015)

Trinity Junction, where the Abbey Hill line joined the original line from Canal Street, is seen here shortly before closure of that line in 1967. The Canal Street line is going straight ahead, with the Abbey Hill line turning to the left. The Caledonian line to Leith crosses over at this point. This contrasts with the 2015 view where all the lines are level and are now cycle paths. (Historic photograph – Kenneth G. Williamson – W. D. Yuill collection)

Soon after Trinity Junction, trains went through Trinity Tunnel, which passed under East Trinity Road. The tunnel mouth is built in a similar style to the Scotland Street Tunnel. (2015)

Trinity is the only station left on the line. The station is now a private residence, and the path ends soon after this point at Trinity Crescent. (2015)

The Penicuik Branch

The paper-making town of Penicuik was served by this North British line from 1872 until 1967, with passenger services ending in 1951.

Turning off the Peebles line at Hawthornden Junction, the 4 ½-mile branch had three intermediate stations at Rosslyn Castle, Auchendinny and Eskbridge, which closed in 1930, and had direct services to Edinburgh Waverley. In the short distance it travelled, the branch crossed the River North Esk five times, including over the ten-arch Firth Viaduct. It also passed through Auchendinny and Old Woodhouselee tunnels.

The branch is now part of the Penicuik to Dalkeith Walkway, which currently ends at Eskbank, following the reopening of the Borders Railway. The 8-mile-long walkway utilises the Penicuik branch and the Peebles line from Hawthornden Junction to Eskbank, passing through Rosewell & Hawthornden and Bonnyrigg stations.

A good round trip is to take the bus from Edinbugh to Penicuik, before walking to Eskbank and then taking the train back to Edinburgh.

The walk starts at the site of Penicuik station, all trace of which has disappeared under a housing estate, as has the paper mill that stood alongside. From the station site the path runs downhill towards the first crossing of the River North Esk. (2015)

This skew bridge carries a minor road over the path. In this view looking back towards Penicuik, the mock level-crossing gates are in place to stop cars accessing the path. Beyond the gates is the site of Eskbrige station, which closed in 1930. (2015)

At Auchendinny, the station house still stands and is in excellent order. (2015)

Auchendinny station is seen here in 1955, four years after passenger services ended. The bay platform track had been lifted by this time. Moving on to 2015 and the site is totally overgrown, but still recognisable. (Historic photograph – Hamish Stevenson)

The River North Esk flows under the Auchendinny Bow String Bridge and the B7026 road bridge, which crosses Auchendinny Tunnel. (2015)

Beyond Auchendinny Tunnel, the path crosses the River North Esk again, on the curved Firth Viaduct, the largest engineering feature on the line. (2015)

This original feature is still in place at Rosslyn Castle station. The partially ruined sixteenth-century Rosslyn Castle stands about a mile away on the edge of Roslin Glen. (2015)

The path climbs to open country and on to the Peebles line after Rosslyn Castle station, giving a fine view towards Rosslyn Chapel and the Pentland Hills. Rosslyn Chapel was founded in 1466 and was originally meant to be part of a much larger church, but this was never built. In more recent times it is famous for being a location in the filming of *The Da Vinci Code*. (2015)

Bonnyrig station still has its platforms and also this British Railways-style totem. At the far end of the platforms, there was once a signal box and level crossing. Beyond the station the line has been built on and the path leads through a housing development before picking it up again. (2015)

The path ends at the new Eskbank station on the Borders Railway. The sign at the end of the footbridge is pointing the way back to Penicuik. (2015)

Lines to Peebles

The borders town of Peebles was served by both the North British Railway from the north and east, and the Caledonian Railway from the west.

The 37-mile North British line turned off the Waverley Route at Hardengreen Junction, south of Eskbank, ran south to Peebles, and then turned east towards Galashiels, rejoining the Waverley Route at Kilnknowe Junction, north of Galashiels.

Opened to a terminus at Pebbles in 1855, and extended to Innerleithan in 1864, and to Galashiels in 1866, a new through station at Peebles was also opened at this time, becoming Peebles East. Including Peebles, there were fourteen stations on the line.

The Caledonian line reached Peebles from Symington on the West Coast Main Line and terminated at Peebles West station. The 20-mile line ran via Biggar and Broughton, and opened to Broughton in 1860 and Peebles in 1864. A link line ran between Peebles West and the North British line, which crossed over the River Tweed.

The line from Symington was the first to close, with passenger services being withdrawn in 1950 and goods from Broughton to Peebles in 1954, with the rest of the line closing in 1966.

The North British line closed completely in 1962, with the exception of the Hardengeen Junction to Hawthornden Junction section, which remained open until 1967, when the Penicuik branch closed.

No trace of the two Peebles stations survives: the realigned A703 covers the site of Peebles East, while Peebles West is now waste ground. I have concentrated on what can be seen in and around Peebles, but other parts of the lines are still traceable.

This plaque marks the site of Peebles East station, now the site of the realigned A703. (2014)

All that is left of the North British station site is this goods office, which is now situated between a car park and a supermarket. (2016)

Looking along the embankment of the line in Peebles, which linked the North British and the Caledonian lines, the remaining abutment of the bridge across the River Tweed can be seen on the far bank. (2014)

Eshiels Tunnel on the eastern outskirts of Peebles is now used as a Sustrans cycle path passing under the A72. The path extends to Innerleithan, using a mix of the old railway and quiet roads. (2014)

Soon after trains left Peebles West, they passed through the 674-yard-long Neidpath Tunnel. It is still possible to walk through the tunnel today. Note the concrete sandbox at the line side. (2014)

Inside, Neidpath Tunnel is initially on a curve before straightening out to the western end. (2014)

Exiting Neidpath Tunnel, trains almost immediately crossed the magnificent Neidpath Viaduct, which spans the River Tweed. This is the view looking towards the tunnel. Note the angle of the stones in the arches. It is possible to walk on from here to Lyne station, where there is a similar but shorter viaduct, or to return to Peebles via the river-side path, which passes below the fourteenth-century Neidpath Castle. (2014)

The Border Counties Railway

Running through desolate countryside, the North British Railways Border Counties line ran for 42 miles from Hexham on the North Eastern Railways line from Newcastle to Carlisle, to the equally desolate Riccarton Junction on the Edinburgh to Carlisle and Waverley Route. Opening in 1862, it was single line throughout. Although future doubling was allowed for in the construction, this failed to happen.

Coal deposits at Plashetts and the need for an alternative route from Newcastle to Edinburgh were the main reasons for the line's construction. The only town of any size on the line was at Bellingham, with all the other stations serving small communities. There was only one station in Scotland, this being at Sauchtree, 3 miles from Riccarton Junction.

Leaving Hexham, the line crossed the River Tyne on the Border Counties Junction Viaduct; the weakness of this structure would hasten the line's end in future years. At Kielder the line crossed the North Tyne on a fine stone viaduct, which can be walked across today.

The hoped-for traffic never materialised, with passenger services withdrawn in 1956, and freight in 1958, although the section from Bellingham to Reedsmouth Junction, where a line branched off to Morpeth, remained open to freight until 1963.

Much of the track bed still exists today, although part of it is now submerged under the Kielder Reservoir and many of the stations have been converted into homes. The line is well worth a visit, as much remains and can be seen from the road; however, bear in mind that the laws differ in England and there is no 'right to roam'.

In this volume I have only covered the Scottish section.

Graeme Blair ponders on the Border Counties line at Riccarton Junction. (2016)

The piers of a bridge across a very wet cutting that the line passes through soon after leaving Riccarton Junction. The Waverley Route can be seen in the distance, just below the line of trees. (2016)

As the line heads downhill towards Sauchtree, you can see just how desolate the countryside is. (2016)

One of a number of sheep creeps over which the track bed passes. Note the two rails clamped together to form a fence post.

The entrance to Sauchtree station off the B6357. The restored station is now run as a bed and breakfast establishment, and the owner has built two homes alongside in a similar style to the station, for himself and his family.

A length of track has been laid through the station on which this ex-Hull oil refinery diesel shunter, with its train of two wagons and a brake van, can run. Out of shot is a former railway worker's cottage, now converted into an engine shed.

Looking south from Sauchtree to the end of the line, there was once a viaduct in the gap just above where the car is standing. The cutting beyond curves away towards the border and the next station, Deadwater.

The Waverley Route and the Opening of the Borders Railway

One of the most controversial closures of the 1960s was the total closure of the Waverley Route, which ran from Edinburgh to Carlisle via Galashiels and Hawick. This steeply graded main line was 98 miles long, and opened between Edinburgh and Hawick in 1849 and Hawick to Carlisle in 1862.

Southbound trains turning onto the Waverley Route at Portobello Junction faced an immediate climb, as steep as 1 in 70 in parts, to Falahill summit, followed by an almost equally steep descent to Galashiels. After Hawick, the climbing started again to Whitrope summit, with sections again as steep as 1 in 75, followed by a 10-mile descent to Newcastleton, mostly at 1 in 75. This section was very challenging for northbound trains due to the many curves on the line.

As well as local trains, the line also carried Anglo-Scottish expresses run jointly by the North British and Midland Railways, running from Edinburgh to London St Pancras. These trains continued to run until the line's closure.

Right to the very end, the line was busy, with Edinburgh Millerhill yard to Carlisle yard fitted freights.

Many branch lines turned off the line and, throughout the 1950s and 1960s, they were gradually closed, until only the main line was left. Closure came in 1969 amid howls of protest – all to no avail. From then on, there were calls to reopen all or part of the line and, finally, in 2015 this happened with the opening of the now renamed Borders Railway, running from Edinburgh to Tweedbank, south of Galashiels.

The fifteen-arch Shankend Viaduct on the climb to Whitrope summit, looking south towards Shankend station and signal box. The station is now a house and the signal box is a holiday home. (2013)

The south portal of Whitrope Tunnel was a few yards short of Whitrope summit, and locomotives would have still been working hard as they exited the tunnel. It is 1,208 yards long, on a curve at each end and on a gradient of 1 in 96. (2013)

Tunnelled beneath marshy ground, Whitrope Tunnel always suffered from water ingress. This finally got the better of it, following years without maintenance, when in 2002 part of the roof just inside the south portal collapsed, leaving this gaping hole. This had been anticipated many years before, prompting the fitting of the steel beams seen at the bottom of the picture, which unfortunately weren't at the part that fell. (2013)

What was Whitrope siding when the line was open is now the headquarters of the Waverley Route Heritage Association, who have laid track from Whitrope summit to the beautifully named Golden Bridge, with the aim of continuing the 2 miles down to Riccarton Junction. This project was started completely from scratch, as there was nothing left following closure. In the two coaches in the bay platform are a café and small museum. (2016)

The track bed curves away from Whitrope through Ninestane Rig Cutting, the first of many curves on the way down to Riccarton Junction. The Bridge 201 sign marks the position of a sheep crossing, one of many on the line. (2013)

Riccarton Junction was a self-contained railway community, only accessible by rail for most of its existence. There were over thirty houses on the site as well as a school, shop and post office to cater for the 150 people who lived and worked there. The top view from the 1960s shows the school master's house and the boarded-up school, while the lower view from 2016 shows both buildings now occupied. Of all the other houses, only the station master's still stands, but in a ruined condition. (Historic photograph – David Crichton)

I am devoting the final section of the book to the opening of the Borders Railway, with six before and after photographs taken when work was started to clear the line and after the tracks were laid.

Bowshank Tunnel between Stowe and Galashiels is on a curve and is 249 yards long. The line crosses the Gala Water, just before entering and just after leaving the tunnel. The tracks in the tunnel are fixed to a solid concrete base rather than on sleepers. (2013/15)

In Galashiels, a supermarket was built very close to the track bed, leaving just enough room for a single track to pass on the way to Tweedbank. Any closer and it would have been going through the wines and spirits section! The line is partially single, with long dynamic loops to allow trains to pass at speed. (2013/15)

Tyne Head is situated 2 miles north of Falahill summit, where the gradient climbs at 1 in 70. Although there was a station here, it has not been reopened. The two photographs show the huge transformation there has been here since work started. The bottom view shows A4 Pacific No. 60009 *Union of South Africa* pulling the Borders Railway opening special, conveying Her Majesty the Queen, the Duke of Edinburgh and Scotland's First Minister to Tweedbank on 9 September 2015. (Before photograph – 2013)